J   733014
915   15.95
Kal
Kalman
Japan, the culture

DATE DUE			
~~TITLE~~ May 8, 97 IU			97235
~~TITLE~~ Nov 30, 98 Tue			
1-50-E			
11-30-98			

JAPAN

the culture

Bobbie Kalman

The Lands, Peoples, and Cultures Series

Toronto
New York

Crabtree Publishing Company

The Lands, Peoples, and Cultures Series
Created by Bobbie Kalman

Writing team
Bobbie Kalman
Janine Schaub
Christine Arthurs
Margaret Hoogeveen

Editor-in-Chief
Bobbie Kalman

Editors
Janine Schaub
Christine Arthurs
Margaret Hoogeveen

Design and layout
Heather Delfino
Margaret Hoogeveen

Printer
Worzalla Publishing Company
Stevens Point, Wisconsin

Illustrations
Halina Below-Spada Back cover, p. 30
John Mantha p. 29
Janine Schaub p. 31

Special thanks
Mrs. Shizuko Kudo for her help.

Photography acknowledgments
Cover: Courtesy of the Royal Ontario Museum
Ian Clifford/E-Side Studios: p. 5; Beverly Deutsch: p. 25(bottom left); Courtesy of Japan Information
Centre: p. 13(bottom), 22(top); Courtesy of Japan National Tourist Organization: p. 7, 9(top right),
10, 17(right), 18(top), 19, 20(top), 21, 22(bottom), 23(right), 24; Margus Jukkum p. 6(top);
Christine McClymont: p. 20(bottom); Gayle McDougall: p. 14(left);
Courtesy of the Royal Ontario Museum: p. 9(middle), 9(bottom, Gift of Sir William Van Horne),
12(Anonymous Gift), 13(top), 26, 27(all three); Larry Rossignol: p. 28(right); Tom Skudra p. 11;
Elias Wakan/Pacific Rim Slide Bank (PRSB): p. 4, 9(upper left), 16, 17(left), 18(circle), 23(left),
25(top left and right), 29; Naomi Wakan/PRSB: Title page, 25(bottom right);
Jamie Worling: p. 6(bottom), 14-15, 15(top and bottom), 28(left).

For baby Eloise

Cataloguing in Publication Data

Kalman, Bobbie, 1947-
    Japan, the culture

(Lands, peoples, and cultures series)
Includes index.
ISBN 0-86505-206-9 (bound), ISBN 0-86505-286-7 (pbk.)
1. Japan - Social life and customs - Juvenile literature.
2. Japan - Civilization - Juvenile literature.
I. Kalman, Bobbie, 1947-   . II. Series.

DS821.J3 1989   j952

Published by
Crabtree Publishing Company

120 Carlton Street	350 Fifth Avenue	73 Lime Walk
Suite 309	Suite 3308	Headington,
Toronto, Ontario	New York	Oxford OX3 7AD

Contents

⛩ The newest and oldest ⛩

Living in Japan is like being part of two contrasting worlds. Modern Japan is an industrialized nation of skyscrapers, busy highways, and the newest high-tech products. Its people dress in the latest styles and seem to love everything modern. The other Japan is a country deeply rooted in its past. It is a quiet world influenced by a love of nature, beauty, art, and ritual.

The Japanese have strong traditions because the vast majority of the people come from one common background and share the same values, beliefs, and customs. There is a particular way of doing things, and only the Japanese fully understand its rules and rituals. Explore Japan's traditions and celebrations. Allow your senses and feelings to discover this delicate, highly developed culture.

The Japanese find western ways fascinating but also love their own old customs. Disneyland, located outside Tokyo, is part of modern Japan. Kimonos, parasols, and festivals belong to traditional Japan.

A love of nature

Nature is the most important theme in Japanese culture. Its beauty and harmony have inspired poets, painters, and musicians. Many Japanese customs and festivals highlight nature's endless cycles. Although most people appreciate nature, the Japanese celebrate every change the seasons bring. In spring they rejoice at the arrival of new flowers, and in autumn they delight in the spectacular colors of the leaves. Even in winter people go to icy, peaceful parks and forests to view the snow.

Cherry blossom viewing

For fifty-one weeks of the year the cherry tree looks ordinary. But when it blooms for one short week in spring, everyone in Japan celebrates. People watch the news eagerly to find out the locations of the more spectacular viewing spots. Thousands of picnickers gather under boughs exploding with pink and white flowers. People are often joyful and sad at the same time because they know that the blossoms are only at their peak for a day or two and then will be gone for another year.

The beauty of wood

For many centuries the Japanese constructed all their buildings from wood. Wood is admired for its natural beauty, its fragrant scent, and its warmth. The Japanese say that a tree has two lives; one while it is growing and another when it has been made into a useful object. Instead of being painted, walls and floors are stained or varnished to preserve wood's natural qualities.

Nature viewing is a favorite pastime all year.

Sculpted gardens

Japanese gardens are works of art created by unseen hands. Wherever there is space, people make a garden. Instead of lawns and flower beds, Japanese gardens contain rocks, pebbles, sand, trees, ponds, and running water. These elements are used to create a miniature world. Rocks represent mountains, a pond stands for an ocean, trees symbolize a forest, and a running stream of water reminds people of a river. In many homes a sliding door opens onto a carefully tended garden. Framed by the doorway, the garden becomes a living picture.

Bonsai

Bonsai, the art of raising miniature trees, is more than a thousand years old. Dwarfed trees are placed in pots, and the branches and roots are constantly pruned. This pruning and lack of space restrict the growth of the trees, causing them to become tiny versions of huge trees. Many *bonsai* are handed down from one generation to the next. One of the oldest was once owned by a *shogun* in the seventeenth century!

(opposite, top) Cherry blossoms remind people that life is beautiful but fragile and brief.

Ikebana

The art of flower arranging is called *ikebana*. Japanese flower arrangements are simple in design, and different flowers and plants are used depending on the season. The flowers and branches are always arranged to symbolize heaven, earth, and people. The main upward branch represents heaven, the branches to the right are people, and the lowest branches on the left stand for the earth.

Preserving nature

Despite the love that individuals may feel for their natural world, the Japanese as a society have not treated their environment with care. Rapid industrialization has caused many kinds of pollution. One of Japan's most challenging tasks is to clean up and preserve the environment that has brought its people so much pleasure.

(above) Gardens are meant to be admired from a distance. The trees, rocks, and water inspire feelings of peace in the viewer. The pebbles are carefully raked, and the verandah is left unpainted to preserve the natural beauty of wood.

7

Over the centuries Japanese artists have developed their own styles of sculpture, painting, and ceramics. Besides conventional arts, the Japanese also specialize in a whole range of crafts that they have developed into fine arts.

Painting with ink

A long time ago Japanese culture was greatly influenced by the Chinese. It is not surprising, then, that early Japanese and Chinese painting styles are both based on the brushstrokes of calligraphy. Japanese ink painting, or *sumi-e*, captures a subject in just a few brushstrokes. Every stroke is crucial to the painting. Like many other Japanese art forms, *sumi-e* has strict rules. Every student must learn how to paint grass before he or she can paint the more complicated cherry blossom.

Story paintings

About nine hundred years ago artists began making story paintings on scrolls. Unlike *sumi-e* paintings, story paintings are colorful and minutely detailed. The most famous are scenes from a novel called *The Tale of Genji*. This novel, written by a Japanese noble-woman named Lady Murasaki, recounts the life of a prince.

One-of-a-kind-ceramic cups

Irregularly shaped, hand-molded ceramic cups are among the most prized pieces of pottery in Japan. Cups made by master potters are cherished both for their usefulness and unique beauty. People admire them for such natural characteristics as a potter's fingerprint in the clay, a bubble in the glaze, an uneven edge, or a dent in the shape. The beauty of one-of-a-kind cups is meant to be experienced by the hands as well as the eyes.

(top left) **An intricately carved ceiling joint**

(center) **A painting of a fan with a scene from The Tale of Genji** *entitled* **"The Royal Visit"**

Handmade paper

Washi is the Japanese word for handmade paper. Many people think it is "rice paper," but it is not made from rice at all. The inner bark from three kinds of plants is pounded into mush and mixed with a solution to produce a thick, pasty substance. This paste is evenly spread onto bamboo mesh screens. When it has dried, sheets of paper are carefully pulled off the screens. Delicately patterned *washi*, such as the background of this page, makes excellent gift wrap.

Origami

Origami is the Japanese art of folding paper into objects without cutting or pasting. Squares of brightly colored or patterned paper are made specifically for *origami*. This crisp paper holds the sharp folds *origami* requires. Birds, animals, fish, flowers, and decorations for gifts can each be folded from a single piece of paper. An *origami* artist can produce animals that move, such as a bird that flaps its wings when its tail is pulled or a frog that hops when its back is tapped! If you want to learn *origami*, find a library book that describes the detailed folding instructions.

Jigsaw joints

The most ingenious feature of Japanese architecture is the way the wooden frame of a building is assembled. The parts of the main frame fit into one another like the pieces of a jigsaw puzzle. Intricately carved pieces of wood lock together at the corners to make secure but flexible joints. A flexible structure is important because Japan suffers from frequent earthquakes. When the ground shakes during an earthquake, the joints are able to withstand the tremors. After an earthquake, a crooked joint can be straightened back into position.

(top right) **This** origami **bird is one piece of paper.**

(bottom) **This century-old ceramic cup decorated with plum blossoms has a beautiful, uneven shape.**

⛩ The treasures of Japan ⛩

The Japanese are anxious to preserve their rich cultural heritage. Masters of traditional art forms such as sword making, *sumi-e* painting, and *Noh* theater are respected for their skills, dedication, and for the beautiful works they create.

Living treasures

Throughout Japan there are thousands of people skilled in the traditional arts. Only a small number of them, however, receive the great honor of being named a "Living National Treasure." This title is reserved for the very best artists. Living National Treasures receive money from the government so they can continue their work. Japan is the only country that recognizes its artists in this way. The government wants to honor them and ensure that they will pass on their valuable skills to the next generation. Dedicated apprentices study for many years learning the techniques of the great masters. Today there are about a hundred Living National Treasures, and a few more artists are honored with the title every year.

(opposite) Mr. Sato proudly wears the special medal given to him for his skill by the emperor.

Kokeshi dolls

Over a hundred years ago the Japanese began carving *kokeshi* dolls. Wooden *kokeshi* dolls have long, slender bodies with large, round heads. After delicate facial features and flower designs are painted on the plain wood, the dolls are coated with a shiny finish. *Kokeshi* dolls are not only admired by the Japanese, they are also prized by doll lovers all over the world.

Woodworkers living in different areas of Japan have developed their own styles of *kokeshi* dolls. If you were to go to the village of Togatta, you could visit Mr. Sato, an eighty-five-year-old doll maker. Although Mr. Sato is now too old to make any more dolls, he is still dedicated to his craft. He instructs his oldest son in the Togatta style of *kokeshi* doll making, just as his father and his father's father have done before him.

(above) In 1794 an artist named Jusaburo Sharaku made over a hundred prints of actors, which are now famous worldwide. The artist in the above photograph continues the tradition of painting these truly Japanese caricatures.

Japanese theater

According to Japanese mythology, theater was first discovered by the gods. The gods then passed on their knowledge to the Japanese. Over the centuries Japanese theater has developed into several rich traditions.

Noh theater

Noh is Japan's oldest form of theater. Performances date back to the fourteenth and fifteenth centuries when plays were put on for the *samurai* and upper classes. *Noh* theater is still performed today. The most famous plays are based on legends and folktales. *Noh* plays often have a dreamlike quality and feature ghosts and spirits. Their timeless themes stress that life is like a wheel. Good and bad fortune come and go in never-ending cycles.

Noh theater is well known for its masks and spectacular costumes. The two main characters change their masks frequently to reveal different emotions. If the heroine is miserable, she wears a mask to show her sadness. When she feels better, she puts on a happy mask. The scenery of a *Noh* play is simple; sometimes the stage is almost bare.

Kabuki

Kabuki theater is also very old. It was first created in the early seventeenth century. *Kabuki* was started by a woman and was originally performed by women actors. Today men play all the parts, even the women's roles. The plays are colorful spectacles performed just as they were two hundred years ago.

Kabuki performances are very long. Some plays last up to six-and-a-half hours! For many, a *Kabuki* play is a social occasion. It is acceptable for members of the audience to

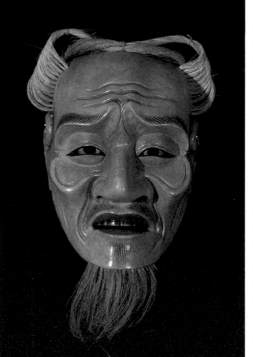

*A wooden **Noh** mask*

make noise and voice their opinions during the performance. People bring their own food and eat while they enjoy the show!

Whereas the *Noh* plays were once performed for the *samurai*, *Kabuki* was the theater for the lower classes. The plays teach a lesson but are meant to be funny. They are often about ordinary people outsmarting members of the upper classes of long ago.

An orchestra, chorus, and dancers are all part of a *Kabuki* play. The chorus sings the story while the performers act out their parts. The actors wear elaborate costumes and heavy makeup and use exaggerated gestures. This may explain why the word *Kabuki* means "to get freaked out!"

Bunraku puppets

Bunraku is a musical puppet theater for adults. *Bunraku* puppets are almost as big as real people. Clothed in black, the puppeteers stand right on stage behind the elaborately dressed puppets. They work in full view of the audience, but the audience soon forgets about them because all attention is focused on the lifelike puppets. It takes three skillful puppeteers to work a puppet: one for the body and right arm, one for the left arm, and one for the feet. A narrator, called a *tayu*, tells the story and says the puppets' lines. A *samisen* accompanies the action. It is a stringed instrument that is played like a guitar.

*(opposite, top) An actor with an unruly mane plays a lion in a **Kabuki** play.*

*(opposite, bottom) Puppeteers dressed in black manipulate large **Bunraku** puppets right on stage.*

Shinto and Buddhism

Most Japanese people practice two religions called Shinto and Buddhism. Both have had a tremendous effect on Japanese culture. Religious and non-religious people alike are influenced by the ideas and rituals of these religions.

Shinto

The Shinto religion is the original religion of the Japanese. According to this ancient belief many gods and goddesses called *kami* populate the world. *Kami* are believed to dwell in all natural creations such as rocks, trees, plants, waterfalls, animals, and the sky. There are also *kami* that protect people from earthquakes, diseases, and fires. The most important *kami* is Amaterasu, the sun goddess. She is the symbol of Japan, and it is believed that all the emperors descended from her. The emperor of Japan is the head of the Shinto religion.

Those who practice Shinto believe that all living things share the same life source. Shinto teaches respect for nature. It also encourages family members to fulfill the hopes of their ancestors and honor the heroes of the past.

Shinto shrines

Shinto shrines are usually built in beautiful settings where worshippers can appreciate nature and feel close to the gods and the spirits of their ancestors. Weddings and baby-blessing ceremonies take place at Shinto shrines. Local shrines honor the *kami* that protect villages and communities. Besides visiting neighborhood shrines, the Japanese also take trips to major Shinto shrines. The most sacred shrine in Japan, located in Ise, is dedicated to Amaterasu.

Japanese people believe that *torii* gates serve as entrances to the spiritual world. These wooden arches are a common sight at Shinto shrines and can also be found in picturesque spots all by themselves. *Torii* gates act as frames through which nature's beauty can be appreciated. Notice the *torii* gate in the picture on page 17. Where else can you find *torii* gates in this book?

(below left) Before entering a Shinto shrine, worshippers rinse their mouths and pour water over their fingertips as acts of purification.

(center) Statues of Buddha and Shinto kami exist side by side in this bamboo forest.

Buddhism

Buddhism is an ancient religion that originally came from India. It spread through China and Korea and eventually came to Japan in the sixth century. Buddhism is based on the teachings of a man named Sakyamuni who became known as the "Awakened One," or Buddha.

Buddhists believe that people are born over and over again and that all their actions have an effect on their next lives. If a person lives a good life, he or she will be rewarded with a better one the next time around. Japanese people believe in ancestor worship and have Buddhist funerals when they die. Many homes have small Buddhist altars with photographs of deceased family members.

Built in 1252, the Amida Buddha is over fourteen meters high. The wooden building that once housed the statue was swept away by a tidal wave.

Zen and *zazen*

There are several kinds of Buddhism. Since the twelfth century the most popular form in Japan has been Zen Buddhism. Zen Buddhism stresses meditation as the way of becoming wise and achieving inner peace. Zen Buddhists practice a special kind of meditation called *zazen*. The purpose of *zazen* is to clear the mind of any thoughts and desires. To help them meditate, Buddhists sit in the lotus position—legs crossed with the soles of their feet facing upward, back straight, and chin tucked in. Priests and monks often face the wall while meditating. Sometimes they fall asleep because meditating can be so relaxing! If they show signs of "dropping off," a monk whacks them on the shoulder with a stick to keep them awake.

When entering a Buddhist temple, people light an incense stick, strike a metal gong, place their hands together, and bow.

Celebrating the past

Hardly a day goes by in Japan without a festival occurring somewhere in the country. Festivals, called *matsuri*, are usually noisy celebrations. They include lively processions, competitions, games, and loud music. Some festivals celebrate the seasons; some celebrate children. A great many have been around for hundreds of years.

The Festival of Ages

Many Japanese festivals focus on the past. One of these is called the Festival of Ages, or *Jidai Matsuri*. It is held at Heian Shrine in Kyoto. From the year 794 to 1185, Kyoto was the capital of Japan. *Jidai Matsuri* celebrates the founding of this ancient capital.

Paraders dress in costumes representing each century since the year 794. Women wear colorful silk kimonos from different time periods. People dressed up as royalty, armored *samurai*, and rice farmers march through the streets of Kyoto. Even the horses are decorated!

*(opposite) This **Jidai Matsuri** participant wears the traditional weapons of the **samurai**: the sword, bow and arrows, and dagger.*

A festival of lanterns

One of the bigger festivals in Japan is the *Bon* Festival, also known as the Festival of Lanterns. The *Bon* Festival honors ancestors. Japanese people believe that the spirits of their dead relatives visit them every year for four days in July. Families gather from all over the country and join together in prayer at the family grave site. On another night of the festival they celebrate the happy return of the spirits by dancing under rows of brightly colored lanterns outside Buddhist temples. The participants, dressed in light summer kimonos called *yukata*, follow the movements of a group of lead dancers. As the people dance in a counterclockwise direction, they resemble a giant, human wheel, representing the Buddhist belief that life is a cycle in which death follows life and rebirth follows death. The dance is meant to welcome and entertain the spirits of their ancestors.

*(bottom left) In the **Jidai Matsuri** parade, a woman shows how firewood was carried in the past.*

*The procession travels through town before returning to the Shinto shrine. The paraders wear headbands called **hachimaki**. Notice the **torii** gate.*

Pine, bamboo, rope, rice straw, lobsters, and seaweed are all used to make New Year decorations. An orange is offered for the spirit of ancestors, folded paper shows the shrine's blessing, and fern represents a wish for prosperity.

⛩ Festivals throughout the year ⛩

The Japanese hold festivals during every season. The year begins with the biggest celebration of all, New Year. People start preparing for it early in December. They pay all their debts, clean their homes, and put up decorations. They buy new clothes for themselves and gifts for their friends. At midnight on New Year's Eve the ropes of the giant bells at the Buddhist temples are pulled 108 times to ring out 108 sins. Everyone visits Shinto shrines sometime during the first week of the year.

New Year's Day is like a birthday party because everyone adds a year to his or her age. People eat a special breakfast and dress in their best kimonos. They open New Year cards. Children receive gifts of money. The day is reserved for visiting family and friends.

New Year decorations

Pine, bamboo, and rope are used in New Year decorations. Pine stands for long life, and bamboo represents flexibility. Rope is a symbol of the sun goddess, Amaterasu. According to legend, Amaterasu hid in a cave after her brother, the wind god, destroyed her rice fields. The sun disappeared from the sky, and the whole world was thrown into darkness. Eight million gods and goddesses gathered outside the cave with a plan to lure out Amaterasu. They began singing and dancing.

When the sun goddess poked her head out to see what was going on, the gods grabbed her. They placed a rope over the entrance of the cave. Since then, ropes appear at the entrances of Shinto shrines and decorate homes at New Year.

Festive flying

In spring the sky is filled with thousands of kites. People spend a great deal of time and energy making great big ones. Some are so large that they need to be skillfully controlled by many people holding several strings. The best place to see spectacular kites is in Nagasakı, where there is a giant kite festival every April. Kite-flying competitions are held in which competitors try to keep their kites in the air as others try to knock them down with their kites.

The huge kite pictured top left is a sure winner!

Summer festivals

In Japan, summertime seems like one big festival. During the warm weather you can see people climbing poles, walking in processions, racing boats, playing tug-of-war, and making a lot of noise. You might even be lucky enough to spot a giant creature, such as the fish pictured above.

Many summer ceremonies are held at night. The participants carry lanterns or torches and parade through the darkness. During *Gion Matsuri*, the most important summer festival, a pageant of fantastic floats on great wooden wheels winds its way through the city of Kyoto.

(above) This giant fish is just one of the spectacular sights that can be seen at a summer festival. You would need a big hook to catch him!

Winter festivals

The Japanese don't stop celebrating in the wintertime. *Yuki Matsuri* and *Kamakura* are examples of two local winter festivals. *Setsubun* celebrates the end of winter.

A winter carnival

Sapporo is the capital city of Hokkaido, an island in northern Japan. On the first day of February residents hold a fantastic snow festival called *Yuki Matsuri*. Trucks transport thousands of loads of snow to the main square. Huge blocks of ice are cut from frozen rivers nearby and are hauled to the site as well. More than two thousand people work together to create massive ice sculptures. They mold and chip. They carve figures of famous people, animals, Buddhas, spaceships, and well-known buildings. Some of the sculptures are enormous! Many people visit Sapporo to view these icy scenes. During the four-day winter carnival there are skiing and skating contests and exciting parades.

Some ice sculptures look like crystal.

Kamakura

Kamakura, meaning "snow hut," is celebrated in the town of Yokote. Young girls, with the help of their parents, choose huge snowdrifts and hollow them out until these big mounds resemble igloos. They cover the floor with a thick straw mat called a *tatami* and place lighted candles on a shelf that has been carved into the wall. The girls leave their shoes outside, sit on the mat in socks and slippers, and wrap themselves in warm quilts. They heat small rice cakes over a little charcoal stove. Parents and neighbors come to visit. The girls offer their guests rice cakes and sips of tea or rice wine. The visitors leave fruit and coins in return. As an added treat, the girls are sometimes allowed to spend the night in their *kamakura*.

Setsubun

Setsubun takes place on February 3. It is a bean throwing festival. The Japanese throw beans to frighten away winter spirits and allow spring spirits to return. Although the Japanese love winter, they look forward to spring blossoms.

(opposite, bottom) To appreciate the immense size of this icy London scene, compare it to the height of the man climbing onto the rooftop. Who is the figure with the pipe supposed to be?

The scary mask represents the winter spirit, which the bean throwers have frightened away.

(below) These girls keep warm by wearing thick kimonos and huddling near a charcoal stove. They have received several pieces of fruit and some coins from family and friends.

21

🕳 Festivals for the young 🕳

The Japanese honor their children by setting aside several days of the year just for them. The numbers three, five, and seven are considered lucky numbers, and are part of these festivals.

Hina Matsuri

Girls look forward to the magic day of March 3, the third day of the third month. Once a year every daughter dresses in her best kimono and sets up a display of her family's collection of historical dolls for *Hina Matsuri*, or the Doll Festival. The dolls represent members of the royal family, with the emperor and empress at the top, and other members of the noble class on lower steps. These works of art, with delicate features and beautiful silk clothes, are very valuable. Some are several hundred years old and have been passed down through many generations. The display also includes miniature furniture and dishes with treats for the dolls. Peach blossoms, a symbol of beauty, decorate the sides of the display. Family members, neighbors, and friends come to view the dolls. The young hosts offer their guests tea and cakes.

Children's Day

Children's Day used to be known as Boys' Day. It is held on May 5, the fifth day of the fifth month. The two symbols for this festival are the carp and the iris. Both stand for strength and courage and remind children to face life's challenges with determination. The carp is strong because, in order to lay its eggs, it must swim upriver against the current. The leaves of the iris are as sharp as the swords used by courageous *samurai* warriors of the past. Boys proudly display *samurai* armor, swords, and warrior dolls. They visit one another to view the displays.

Each carp flying from this pole stands for one member of the family. Whom do the two largest ones represent?

These young girls are dressed in their best kimonos for Shichi-go-san. *How old is each child?*

On Children's Day carp made of paper or cloth are hung on bamboo poles outside every home. Each member of the family is represented by one carp.

The *Shichi-go-san* Festival

Shichi means seven, *go* means five, and *san* means three. If you were seven, five, or three years old in Japan, you would look forward to November 15. It is a special day of celebration for children of these ages.

On the day of *Shichi-go-san*, children dress in traditional clothes. Boys wear wide trousers called *hakama*, and girls wear their best kimonos. Families go to local shrines and pray to their patron *kami* for the good health of the children. The children ring a giant bell, clap their hands to get the attention of the *kami*, and also recite a brief prayer. Afterwards there are parties with family and friends, and the children receive many presents. *Shichi-go-san* is a lot like a birthday party!

The *Tanabata* Festival

The *Tanabata* Festival is on July 7, the seventh day of the seventh month. It celebrates the love between two celestial stars, the Weaver Princess and the Shepherd, who fell in love and were punished for neglecting their heavenly duties. They were separated by the Milky Way and only allowed to meet on this one day each year.

In honor of the two stars, young people parade through the streets carrying lanterns, colorful streamers, and bamboo poles decorated with strips of paper on which love poems have been written. Young girls hope the wind will carry their poems and wishes to the Weaver Princess. In the past they asked her to help them become better weavers. Today they hope the Weaver Star will help them improve their calligraphy.

(opposite) A young girl admires one of her friend's priceless dolls during **Hina Matsuri.**

Ancient robes

As much as the Japanese love modern clothes, they treasure their traditional kimonos. The kimono is a floor-length silk robe embroidered with intricate designs. This garment, which has no buttons or zippers, is held together by a sash at the waist. For two thousand years Japanese men, women, girls, and boys have worn many varieties of this lovely robe. On New Year's Day, people all over Japan wear their best kimonos to Shinto shrines.

Seasonal kimonos

Kimonos are nearly all made to a standard size, style, and cut. They differ only in color and quality. Light and comfortable kimonos called *yukata* are worn in summer, and cozy flannel kimonos called *nemaki* are worn in winter. There are formal kimonos in dark shades for men and colorfully embroidered kimonos for women. Japanese artisans are well known for their creation of exquisitely patterned kimonos. The most complicated designs are woven on hand-operated looms.

How to put on a kimono

The formal women's kimono is the most difficult to put on. The first layer is a slip called a *nagajuban.* *Tabi*, special socks that separate the big toe from the rest are put on at the same time. The outer kimono, which is made of heavier silk, comes next. It has sleeves that hang down to the ground. The kimono is always folded with the left side over the right. Instead of a light sash, a woman puts on an *obi*, which is a wide band of embroidered silk that wraps very tightly around her waist area. A woman in a kimono may look beautiful, but she is not very comfortable. It is difficult to breathe, lift the arms, bend over, or take normal-sized steps.

(above) Women wear their finest kimonos to Shinto shrines on New Year's Day. Fur stoles keep their necks warm. Notice the elaborately tied obi.

(opposite, top right) When a woman is dressed in her best kimono, she usually wears a beautiful hairstyle to complement her outfit.

(bottom right) On festival days boys often wear wide-legged trousers called hakama.

(left) This ancient kimono, displayed on a manne-quin, has twelve layers. Kamon, or family crests, are part of the pattern. Read about kamon on page 29.

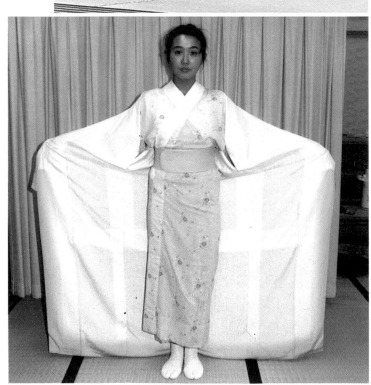

The **nagajuban** *goes under the kimono. Wooden sandals called* **geta** *are worn over socks called* **tabi**.

The tea ceremony

There is much more to the Japanese tea ceremony than just drinking a cup of tea. It is a ritual that involves a series of actions carried out in simple and quiet surroundings. It takes several years to master the art of making, serving, and taking Japanese tea correctly.

A long tea-drinking tradition

Tea drinking in Japan dates back to the Middle Ages when the Japanese were introduced to tea by the Chinese. At first, tea was used by Zen priests to help them stay awake during meditation. Over the centuries all kinds of rules were developed for carrying out the tea ceremony.

The tea ceremony is more popular today than ever before. Not only does it teach people about Japanese culture, it also helps them think in a disciplined way. Some people say that learning the tea ceremony is like learning the steps of a complicated and elegant dance. The host and guests concentrate throughout the long ceremony, and everyone involved knows in advance what they are expected to do.

A formal noontime tea

There are many variations of the tea ceremony. The way each one is performed depends on the occasion or time of day. A formal noontime tea ceremony is performed by a host for up to five guests. The guests are invited to a special tea house surrounded by a garden. When they arrive, they must wait fifteen minutes in a small room near the garden gate. An attendant leads them to an outdoor waiting area. The host and guests greet one another with silent bows and walk together toward the tea room, admiring the gardens along the way. After cleansing their hands and removing their shoes, they file into the tea room headfirst through a small door. The last person shuts the door with a bang and locks it. This is a signal to the host that he or she may light the charcoal fire in the fire pit.

Lanterns light the way to this tea house located in a natural setting among trees and bushes.

The host kneels as she ladles hot, thick tea into uniquely shaped cups.

Preparing the tea

While the coals grow hot, and the water in the kettle boils, the guests are served a small snack. After it is eaten, the host collects the dishes in silence. Keeping silent is meant to bring the feelings of the host and guests into harmony. The host makes a thick, green brew using the hot water and powdered tea. The tea resembles a paste. The guests concentrate on every movement the host makes. The group holds a brief, formal conversation while sipping the tea. Each guest admires the beautiful cups and utensils. Then everyone is silent again, and the fire is smothered. A thin, frothy tea is served at the end, drawing the ceremony to a close.

The sweets served at the tea ceremony look exquisite and taste delicious.

Japanese ways

Pet cemeteries
In some areas of Japan people give their cats and dogs funerals and bury them in special pet cemeteries. Sculptures of animals and wooden plaques containing prayers decorate the well-tended grave sites.

The big gusher!
Mount Fuji is the most famous mountain in Japan. *Fuji* means "gushing out" in the language of the Ainu, the first inhabitants of Japan. It is believed that the Ainu gave the volcano this name because they witnessed a huge eruption ten thousand years ago!

Belly to belly
Many people associate love with the heart. For the Japanese the stomach is the center of the emotions. Instead of having heart-to-heart talks, the Japanese "open their stomachs" for a good conversation. And when a person wants to compliment a friend for being generous, he or she might say, "You are potbellied." Potbellied does not mean a person is chubby. It means he or she is "big-hearted."

Bibbed statues
Small stone statues wearing red cloth bibs and bonnets are a common sight in Japan. These statues represent the all-loving Buddhist guardian deity named Jizo. Jizo looks after the souls of children who have died. Bonnets and bibs are placed on Jizo statues in loving memory of these children.

Model officers
Japan has an army of life-sized police officer models that stand by the side of the road or sit in patrol cars. These realistic models are meant to keep people from speeding along the highways. Recently life-sized photographs of police have been added to this model brigade.

An upside-down frown
Have you heard the expression, "A smile is just a frown turned upside down?" This saying is particularly true in Japan. When a person smiles, it is not always a sign of happiness. A smile is often used to hide other emotions such as embarrassment, confusion, and anger.

Bowing
Bowing is one way the Japanese show courtesy and respect to others. In Japan, people bow instead of shaking hands. A bow may be a nod of the head or a full bend from the waist. When meeting the emperor, people kneel down with their hands outstretched and almost touch the floor with their heads.

Try these activities

Samurai helmets

In ancient times *samurai* warriors protected themselves by wearing armor and fearsome helmets. The helmets were specifically designed to frighten the enemy. Using cardboard, construction paper, aluminum foil, and paint, make a *samurai* helmet of your own. Create a design that would scare the most frightening *samurai*. Wear your helmet while performing a particularly difficult task.

Sets of nests

The Japanese are experts at making nests but not with sticks and bits of string! A nest is a set of several objects of the same shape in many different sizes. Each one fits neatly within the next, which is slightly larger in size. Four stacking tables, from small to large, are an example of nested objects. Find several boxes or make some from construction paper, each one fitting into the next, and create a set of nested boxes. Cover them with origami paper or handmade paper called *washi*.

The importance of "nothingness"

The Japanese appreciate empty space. In a painting the white space is as important as the painted areas. When a Japanese person admires a tree, he or she also admires the shapes and areas of sky among the branches. Try looking at a painting or scenery in this way. You may be surprised to find out how different it looks from this new point of view. Now try this experiment with your sense of hearing. Change your idea of "nothingness" into "somethingness!"

Design a frightening **samurai** *helmet.*

Family crests

The *kamon* is a Japanese family crest. The symbol used is often a favorite plant, animal, or a simple design such as a cross or a letter. In the early days of Japan, *kamon* were embroidered on the garments of men who were involved in hand-to-hand combat. It was the only way to identify one's own fighters from those of the enemy. The *samurai* used *kamon* to mark their clan's belongings such as carriages, boxes, lanterns, and rooftiles. Today *kamon* are used as designs on kimonos and all kinds of decorative objects. Choose a symbol that is important to you and design your own distinctive *kamon*. The examples on this page will help you.

A cherry blossom tree

Even though the cherry tree blooms only once a year, you can make an artificial tree that will decorate your classroom or home all year round. Find a branch that has fallen from a tree. Remove all the leaves and then prop the branch up in a pot filled with earth. Paint the branches brown or black to resemble the cherry tree's dark bark. Make tiny blossoms from white or pink tissue paper. Cut out circles, pinch the centers, and glue the flowers to the branches. Unlike a real cherry tree, your tree will not lose its blossoms after a few days. The beautiful blooms can decorate your room or classroom for as long as you wish.

Make a kimono

Make the kimono pictured below by following these steps. Use two kinds of Japanese paper. You can also use gift wrap for the outside and tissue paper for the lining.

1. Measure the parts of the kimono shown on this page—the length and width of the body, sleeves, and belt. Use these measurements for your kimono.
2. Cut a rectangular piece of patterned paper that is the length of the body of the kimono and twice the width shown. Cut a piece of one-colored Japanese paper or tissue paper the same size.
3. Paste the wrong sides of the two pieces together.
4. Fold the body of the kimono lengthwise towards the middle. You can do this by dividing the width of your paper into four exact parts. Mark these divisions lightly at the top and bottom of your paper. Fold one quarter in towards the middle. Now do the same on the other side. Fold back the collar and left side of skirt into small triangles to reveal the lining of the kimono.
5. Cut one long rectangle for the sleeves as shown.
6. Make the neck piece of the kimono from another rectangle of colored paper twice the length of the width of this kimono. Fold as shown.

  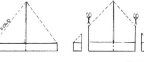

7. Insert the neck piece and fasten it with a dab of glue. Make a belt, or *obi*, from the same-colored paper and glue the ends to the back of the kimono.
8. To finish, glue the body onto the sleeves.

Use your own kimono to decorate a gift or your binder. Frame it and hang it on your wall. Get your friends to make kimonos and put up a kimono display on your classroom bulletin board. Glue your kimono onto a card, write a haiku poem inside, and send it to a friend.

Haiku

Haiku was developed by the Japanese in the seventeenth century. Originally these short poems were about nature. Today, people write about almost any subject. Haiku appeals to the reader's emotions. You may read a poem and feel happy or sad without knowing why!

Haiku is the most popular form of Japanese poetry, but people all over the world enjoy writing these short poems. They are only three lines long and contain seventeen syllables. The first line has five, the second has seven, and the last also has five. The numbers three, five, and seven are important in haiku poetry because they are considered lucky numbers. The following poems were written by children who have discovered the joy of haiku! Try writing your own haiku poetry.

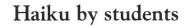

Haiku by students

I flutter and dive
swinging my tail in the breeze.
A kite lives for wind.
Andrew Mitani, age 12

Death in a blossom.
losing a life of wonder
from a love-lost girl.
Blair Livingstone, age 11

Turtles in a tank
swimming among plastic plants
wishing for a pond.
Samantha Crabtree, age 10

Glossary

Ainu - The first group of people to live in Japan, who now live on the northern island of Hokkaido

ancestors - People from whom one is descended

apprentice - A person who works for an artisan in order to learn a trade or art

art form - Work that is especially beautiful or meaningful. Sword making is a Japanese art form.

calligraphy - The art of fine handwriting. In Japan calligraphers use special ink, paper, and brushes.

celestial - Relating to the sky

ceramic - A type of pottery that is fired at temperatures higher than 500°C

chorus - A group of people that sings or speaks together at the same time

culture - The customs, beliefs, and arts of a distict group of people

cycle of life - The continuous course that life takes, including birth, death, and rebirth

deity - A god or goddess

devotion - A strong attachment

embroidery - Intricate designs sewn with a needle and thread

heritage - The customs, achievements, and history passed on from earlier generations; tradition

industrialization - The term used to describe a shift from an agricultural society to one that produces goods in factories

incense - A substance that produces a sweet-smelling smoke when burned

kimono - A loose-fitting, wide-sleeved Japanese robe that is tied with a sash

master - A person of great skill or ability; an expert

meditation - The act of emptying the mind of all thought in order to achieve a state of inner peace

Milky Way - A galaxy made up of more than a hundred billion stars, appearing as a bright white path across the sky. Our solar system is part of the Milky Way.

mythology - A collection of legends or stories that try to explain mysterious events or ideas

procession - A group of people walking in lines as part of a ceremony. Processions are common in Japanese festivals.

purification - The act of becoming clean. Before entering a Shinto shrine, the Japanese purify themselves by washing their hands and rinsing their mouths.

ritual - A formal custom in which several steps are faithfully followed

samurai - The warriors who lived in ancient Japan

shogun - A powerful man in ancient Japan who carried out all laws on behalf of the emperor. Shogun means the "emperor's general."

shrine - A structure that is dedicated to a deity. Those who believe in Shinto visit shrines that are dedicated to spirits called *kami*.

syllable - A word or part of a word pronounced with a single uninterrupted sounding of the voice

symbol - Something that represents or stands for something else

tatami - A standard-sized mat woven from rice straw

temple - A sacred house of worship. Buddhists visit temples to practice their religious rituals.

western - The term used to describe people from the western part of the world, especially Europe and North America, as opposed to people from Asia, such as the Chinese and Japanese

Index

56789 WP Printed in the U.S.A. 876543